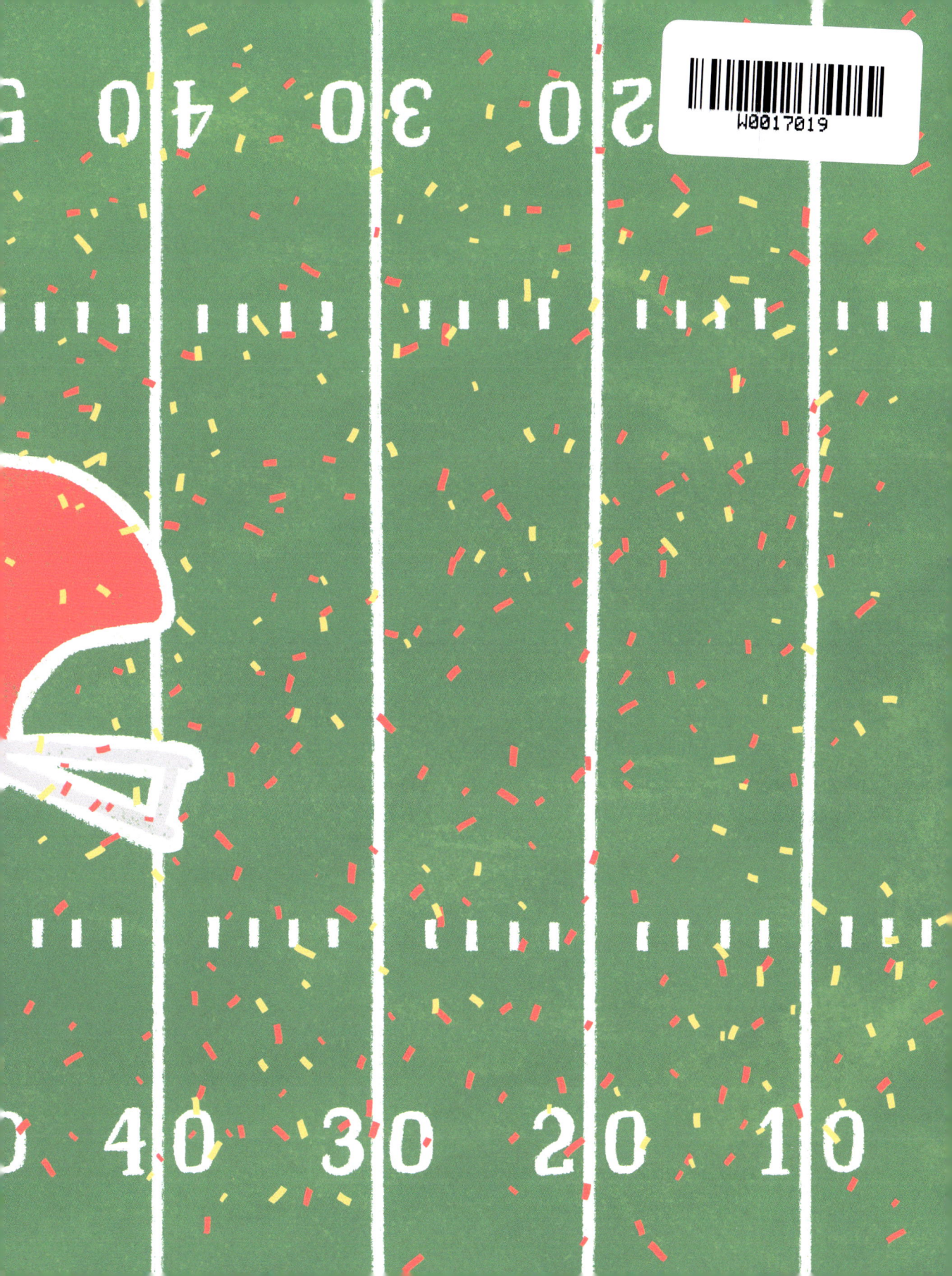

*Little People,* **BIG DREAMS**™

# PATRICK MAHOMES

Written by
Maria Isabel Sánchez Vegara

Illustrated by
Guilherme Karsten

Frances Lincoln
Children's Books

Little Patrick was a bouncy boy from Texas who
seemed destined to play baseball. His father was a
professional player, and Patrick never missed a game.
He dreamed of following in his dad's footsteps.

Besides perfecting his pitching and batting, Patrick picked
up many skills from his dad. Hanging out at the ballpark,
he learned how to be a kind teammate, a respectful leader,
and a good friend.

Patrick was in elementary school when his parents decided to split up. He and his brother, Jackson, stayed with their mom.

To make sure they had everything they needed, she worked extra shifts. But she still found time to be Patrick's number-one fan.

As he grew, Patrick mastered many sports:
baseball, basketball, football, golf . . .
even table tennis! Each sport gave him the chance
to learn something new and become a better athlete.

By the end of high school, he was still playing baseball but had fallen in love with football. Many colleges were impressed by his skills as a pitcher and quarterback, yet Patrick had already made up his mind . . .

After his second year at Texas Tech University, he decided to put all his energy into football. Soon, Patrick was smashing team records with his throws, determined to reach the big leagues and turn pro.

He was twenty-one when he left college to join the Kansas City Chiefs—part of the NFL! Patrick had to wait until the end of his first season to play. But in just two games, he showed that he should be the starting quarterback.

In his second season, Patrick was named the league's Most Valuable Player. Just two years later, he led the Chiefs to their first Super Bowl win in fifty years.

They were the most formidable team, and Kansas City was bursting with pride!

The next year, Patrick's team lost the NFL Championship to the Buccaneers and their legendary quarterback Tom Brady. It was a sad day for Patrick, yet he knew that from every experience there was a lesson to be learned.

The Chiefs reached the final again two seasons later.
They were behind against the Eagles when Patrick felt pain
in his ankle. Still, he refused to leave the field. He knew
his team relied on him to win!

Patrick was already a football legend and had shattered most NFL records when he won his third Super Bowl in five years. Everyone was eager to see where his powerful arm, quick legs, and surprising throws would take him next.

On this amazing journey, Brittany—his high-school sweetheart—has always been by his side.

9:35

Together, they help improve children's lives through Patrick's foundation: *15 and the Mahomies.*

And that is how Patrick—the little boy who dreamed of pitching baseballs—became the world's greatest quarterback. He proves that sometimes the most incredible victories come from the most unexpected dreams.

# PATRICK MAHOMES

(Born 1995)

2016

2019

Patrick Lavon Mahomes II was born in Tyler, Texas. His father, Pat Mahomes, was a professional baseball pitcher who played in the major leagues. Young Patrick loved baseball and dreamed that one day he'd play professionally, too. But baseball wasn't the only sport he loved—through high school and into college, Patrick also played football. While at Texas Tech University, he became known for his exceptionally long throw and record number of touchdowns. During this time, Patrick decided it was time to leave baseball behind and follow a new dream: playing in the National Football League. Not long after, he was asked to join the Kansas City Chiefs and in 2018 became their starting quarterback. Over the next five years, he led the Chiefs to Super Bowl victory three times and was named the league's

2023                    2024

Most Valuable Player twice! Patrick has broken numerous records, including being the fastest NFL quarterback to reach 25,000 career passing yards. Passionate about equality for all, he has spoken up against racism and discrimination and aims to use his fame to "make the world a better place." Through his foundation, Patrick is dedicated to improving children's health and wellbeing, and helps run a program which encourages children to develop a love for reading. His teammate in life is his wife, Brittany, an entrepreneur and former professional soccer player. Together, they are parents and business partners, having co-founded the women's soccer team Kansas City Current. Patrick's journey reminds us that however our dreams change, it's our determination to achieve them that counts.

Want to find out more about **Patrick Mahomes**?

Have a read of this great book:

*Sports Heroes: Patrick Mahomes: The Story of the Football Superstar*

by Hannah Dolan and Guy Harvey

Published by Peter Marley · Edited by Molly Mead
Designed by Sasha Moxon and Izzy Bowman
Production by Robin Boothroyd
Manufactured in Bosnia and Herzegovina
1 3 5 7 9 8 6 4 2

Photographic acknowledgments (pages 28-29, from left to right): 1. Texas Tech quarterback Patrick Mahomes throws out the ceremonial first pitch before a baseball game between the Toronto Blue Jays and the Texas Rangers on Friday, May 13, 2016, in Arlington, Texas © Associated Press Photo/Tony Gutierrez via Alamy Stock Photo. 2. Kansas City Chiefs v New England Patriots: Patrick Mahomes #15 of the Kansas City Chiefs throws the ball during warm ups before a game against the New England Patriots at Gillette Stadium on December 8, 2019 in Foxborough, Massachusetts © Adam Glanzman/Stringer via Getty Images. 3. Kansas City Chiefs quarterback Patrick Mahomes (15) leaves the field with his wife, Brittany, after the NFL Super Bowl 57 football game, Sunday, Feb. 12, 2023, in Glendale, Ariz. The Chiefs defeated the Philadelphia Eagles 38-35 © Matt Slocum/Associated Press Photo via Alamy Stock Photo. 4. Super Bowl LVIII – San Francisco 49ers v Kansas City Chiefs: Patrick Mahomes #15 of the Kansas City Chiefs holds the Lombardi Trophy after defeating the San Francisco 49ers 25-22 during Super Bowl LVIII at Allegiant Stadium on February 11, 2024 in Las Vegas, Nevada © Jamie Squire/Staff via Getty Images.

# Collect the *Little People*, **BIG DREAMS**™ series:

| | | | | | | | | |
|---|---|---|---|---|---|---|---|---|
| FRIDA KAHLO | COCO CHANEL | MAYA ANGELOU | AMELIA EARHART | AGATHA CHRISTIE | MARIE CURIE | ROSA PARKS | AUDREY HEPBURN | EMMELINE PANKHURST |
|  ELLA FITZGERALD | ADA LOVELACE | JANE AUSTEN | GEORGIA O'KEEFFE | HARRIET TUBMAN | ANNE FRANK | MOTHER TERESA | JOSEPHINE BAKER | L. M. MONTGOMERY |
| JANE GOODALL | SIMONE DE BEAUVOIR | MUHAMMAD ALI | STEPHEN HAWKING | MARIA MONTESSORI | VIVIENNE WESTWOOD | MAHATMA GANDHI | DAVID BOWIE | WILMA RUDOLPH |
|  DOLLY PARTON | BRUCE LEE | RUDOLF NUREYEV | ZAHA HADID | MARY SHELLEY | MARTIN LUTHER KING JR. | DAVID ATTENBOROUGH | ASTRID LINDGREN | EVONNE GOOLAGONG |
| BOB DYLAN | ALAN TURING | BILLIE JEAN KING | GRETA THUNBERG | JESSE OWENS | JEAN-MICHEL BASQUIAT | ARETHA FRANKLIN | CORAZON AQUINO | PELÉ |
| ERNEST SHACKLETON | STEVE JOBS | AYRTON SENNA | LOUISE BOURGEOIS | ELTON JOHN | JOHN LENNON | PRINCE | CHARLES DARWIN | CAPTAIN TOM MOORE |
|  HANS CHRISTIAN ANDERSEN | STEVIE WONDER | MEGAN RAPINOE | MARY ANNING | MALALA YOUSAFZAI | ANDY WARHOL | RUPAUL | MICHELLE OBAMA | MINDY KALING |
| IRIS APFEL | ROSALIND FRANKLIN | RUTH BADER GINSBURG | MARILYN MONROE | KAMALA HARRIS | ALBERT EINSTEIN | CHARLES DICKENS | YOKO ONO | MICHAEL JORDAN |

NELSON MANDELA | PABLO PICASSO | AMANDA GORMAN | GLORIA STEINEM | FLORENCE NIGHTINGALE | HARRY HOUDINI | J.R.R. TOLKIEN | ELVIS PRESLEY | NEIL ARMSTRONG

ALEXANDER VON HUMBOLDT | NIKOLA TESLA | WILMA MANKILLER | MARCUS RASHFORD | LAVERNE COX | MAE JEMISON | DWAYNE JOHNSON | HELEN KELLER | ANNA PAVLOVA

QUEEN ELIZABETH | TERRY FOX | HEDY LAMARR | SHAKIRA | FREDDIE MERCURY | LEWIS HAMILTON | LOUIS PASTEUR | PRINCESS DIANA | DAVID HOCKNEY

VANESSA NAKATE | OLIVE MORRIS | KING CHARLES | MOZART | STEVE IRWIN | JÜRGEN KLOPP | LEO MESSI | SALLY RIDE | TENZING NORGAY

KYLIE MINOGUE | BEYONCÉ | TAYLOR SWIFT | RAFA NADAL | USAIN BOLT | SIMONE BILES | STAN LEE | LEONARD COHEN | VINCENT VAN GOGH

MARY KOM | SALVADOR DALÍ | ANTOINE DE SAINT-EXUPÉRY | DAVID BECKHAM | KATHERINE JOHNSON | YAYOI KUSAMA

PATRICK MAHOMES | ROALD DAHL

Scan the QR code for free activity sheets, teachers' notes and more information about the series at www.littlepeoplebigdreams.com

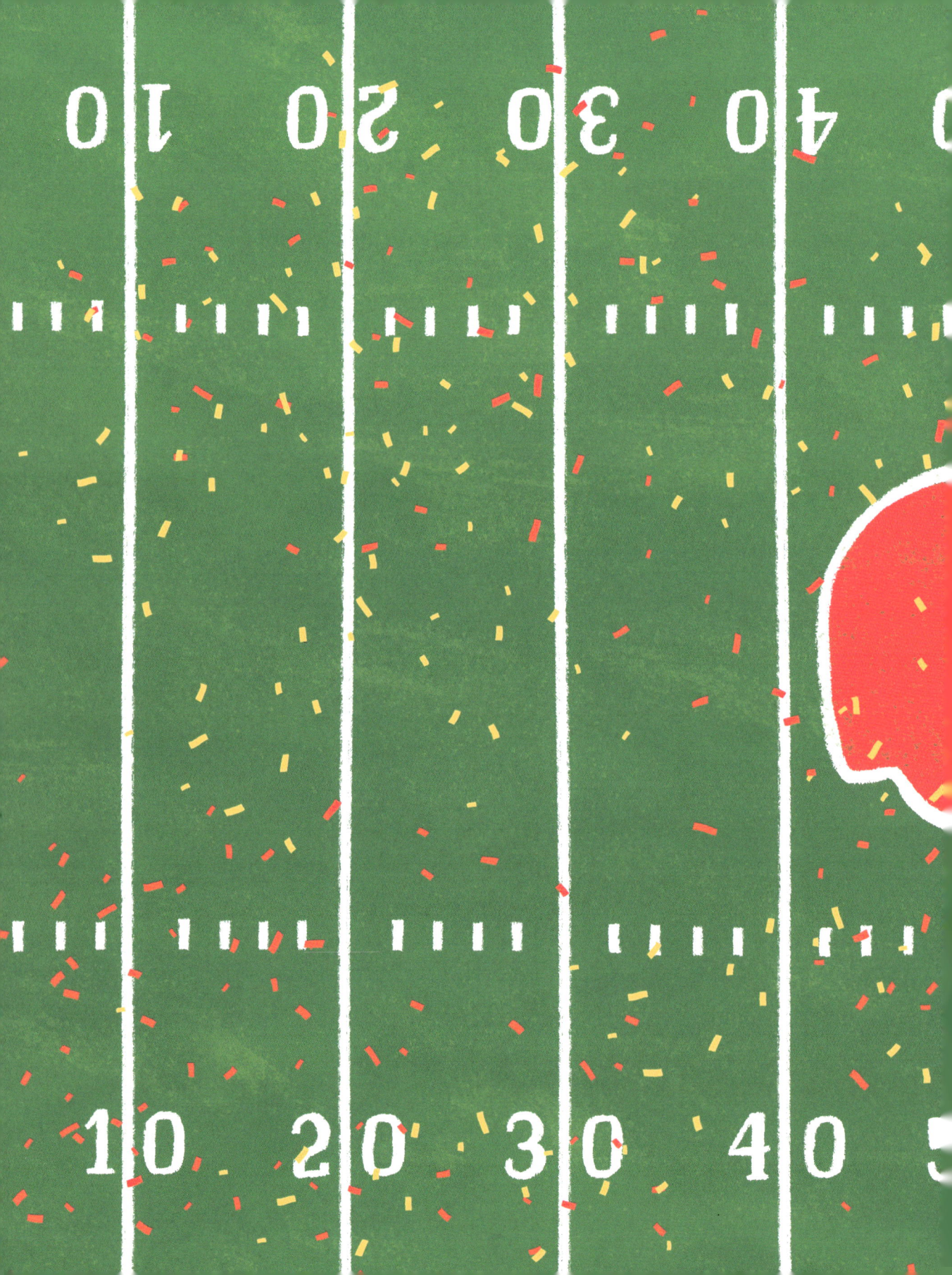